Unpa

Coaching

Mindsets

Collaboration Between Principals and Coaches

Jacy Ippolito and Rita M. Bean

1400 Centrepark Blvd., Ste 1000
West Palm Beach, FL 33401
717.845.6300
email: pub@learningsciences.com
learningsciences.com

Printed in the United States of America

22   21   20   19   18   1   2   3   4   5

Library of Congress Control Number: 2018937226

Publisher's Cataloging-in-Publication Data
provided by Five Rainbows Cataloging Services

Names: Ippolito, Jacy, author. | Bean, Rita M., author.

Title: Unpacking coaching mindsets : collaboration between principals and coaches / Jacy Ippolito [and] Rita Bean.

Description: West Palm Beach, FL : Learning Sciences, 2018.

Identifiers: LCCN 2018937226 | ISBN 978-1-943920-27-3 (pbk.)

Subjects: LCSH: Education. | Learning. | Effective teaching. | Educational leadership. | Educational psychology. | School administrators. | BISAC: EDUCATION / Professional Development. | EDUCATION / Teaching Methods & Materials / General. | EDUCATION / Leadership.

Classification: LCC LB1025.3 .I66 2018 (print) | LCC LB1025.3 (ebook) | DDC 371.102--dc23.

Cover art by Elaine Ippolito.

Table of Contents

Chapter 4

Chapter 5

Chapter 6

About the Authors

 **Jacy Ippolito** is an associate professor and department chair of secondary and higher education in the School of Education at Salem State University, Salem, Massachusetts. Jacy's research, teaching, and consulting focus on the intersection of adolescent and disciplinary literacy, literacy coaching, teacher leadership, and school reform. Results of Jacy's research and consulting work can be found in many journals including the *Journal of Adolescent & Adult Literacy*, the *Journal of School Leadership*, *Professional Development in Education*, *The Learning Professional*, and *The Elementary School Journal*. His recent books include *Investigating Disciplinary Literacy* (2017), *Cultivating Coaching Mindsets* (2016), and *Adolescent Literacy in the Era of the Common Core* (2013). Jacy completed undergraduate degrees in English and psychology at the University of Delaware before completing his master's and doctorate in language and

literacy at the Harvard Graduate School of Education. Prior to his work in higher education, Jacy taught in the Cambridge Public Schools, Cambridge, Massachusetts.

Rita M. Bean is professor emerita, University of Pittsburgh, Department of Instruction and Learning. Rita has focused her research on the role and impact of reading specialists and literacy coaches in schools. She has participated in several national studies that have resulted in national position statements about the roles of reading specialists and literacy coaches (International Literacy Association). Results of her research have been published in journals and books. Recent books include *Cultivating Coaching Mindsets* (2016), *The Reading Specialist: Leadership and Coaching for the Classroom, School, and Community* (2015), and a co-edited volume, *Best Practices of Literacy Leaders: Keys to School Improvement* (2011). She received her BS from Edinboro University of Pennsylvania and her master's degree and PhD from the University of Pittsburgh. Rita received the University of Pittsburgh's Distinguished Teacher Award and the Chancellor's Distinguished Service Award for her community and outreach efforts to improve literacy. In 2009, she was elected to the Reading Hall of Fame and served as its president from 2015 to 2017.

Introduction

In 2016, we published a book titled *Cultivating Coaching Mindsets: An Action Guide for Literacy Leaders (CCM)*. The book was designed to be a guide for coaches, specialized literacy professionals, principals, and other school leaders—all of whom share responsibility for leading literacy teaching and learning in schools. The book introduced a new framework for thinking and working like a coach, and illustrated the many ways that coaches, and literacy leaders more broadly, can support professional learning around literacy instruction.

In response to positive feedback, we have created this companion to support literacy leaders in schools and serve as a study guide and resource for those preparing to become literacy leaders. We believe that this resource serves multiple purposes and audiences.

- **Reference Guide.** This booklet highlights major points from *Cultivating Coaching Mindsets*, providing those who have read it with a brief reminder of critical concepts, strategies, and essential questions. We see this resource as a "hallway" or "on-the-fly" guide, something that a coach or principal might tuck under their arm as they move from classroom to classroom, and meeting to meeting. Moreover, for those who have not yet read *CCM* (or have only skimmed specific chapters), this resource acts as an introduction and way of deciding which sections of the longer book might be of most interest.

○ **Partnership Builder.** This resource is designed to be a conversation starter for principals and coaches/specialized literacy professionals. Oftentimes, principals and coaches are working on similar goals for schoolwide improvement of literacy teaching and learning. However, because of busy schedules and too many competing demands, principals and coaches do not always take the time to sit down and collaboratively craft a vision for coaching work and schoolwide literacy instruction. This resource speaks directly to coaches and principals as *partners* in leading literacy improvement efforts. Each section of the resource ends with specific uses, as well as "reflection" questions that prompt principals and coaches to consider ways in which their independent and shared work can further schoolwide goals. Our aim is to strengthen principal and coach relationships in service of continual improvement.

○ **Study Guide.** With the widespread adoption of *CCM* for graduate coursework related to the preparation of instructional coaches, principals, and other specialized literacy professionals, this booklet might serve as a study guide and quick reference tool for those being prepared to serve in these roles. *Cultivating Coaching Mindsets* has been featured in International Literacy Association position statements, and in the Standards for the Preparation of Literacy Professionals 2017. Given this, the book will continue to be a mainstay in higher education settings, and thus we have created the current resource with an eye toward serving those being prepared as coaches, literacy specialists, and principals.

Finally, a note about the tone and style of this resource, as well as a few unique features. We have created this resource for ease of use and quick reference, which means that we use informal language and speak directly to you—the professionals who need this resource the most! We also have included blank, lined pages in the back of the book to take notes and record the results of collaborative conversations among principals, specialized literacy professionals, and other colleagues. Moreover, at the end of most sections, we include "notes from the authors" (denoted by our initials), in which we share quick personal comments and thoughts related to each of the topics at hand.

We thoroughly enjoyed collaborating on the creation of this resource. We see it as an extension of the conversation we began when we started writing *Cultivating Coaching Mindsets*. Now, we encourage you to reach out to us directly to "keep the conversation going" too! Feel free to let us know about your literacy leadership challenges and successes, and if/how *CCM* and this resource have supported you. You can connect with us directly via email (Jacy Ippolito: jippolito@salemstate.edu and Rita Bean: ritabean@pitt.edu). We hope that this resource serves you well.

-Jacy and Rita

CHAPTER 1

Framework for Thinking and Acting Like a Coach

Whether or not you hold the formal title of "coach," you will be well-served by thinking and working like a coach if you are supporting adult professional learning in schools.

The framework at the heart of *Cultivating Coaching Mindsets* (2016) helps all educators consider the habits of mind and ways of working that support efforts to design and foster a collaborative culture of ongoing professional learning (see Figure 1.1). Following are four primary ways of thinking and working.

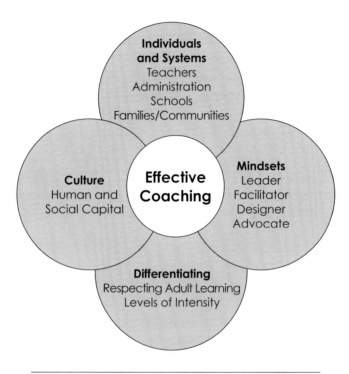

Figure 1.1: Framework for Thinking and Working Like a Coach.

1. Thinking About Individuals and Systems Simultaneously

While one-on-one coaching and individualized professional learning experiences are powerful, if we only engage teachers individually we are missing opportunities to build systems-level capacity. Savvy literacy leaders need to balance one-on-one, small-group, and large-group professional learning experiences to improve teaching and learning systemwide.

2. **Adopting Coaching Mindsets and Roles**

Literacy leaders are well-served by simultaneously thinking and working as:

- ○ Leaders setting professional learning targets and agendas; bridging one-on-one, small-group, and large-group experiences; differentiating adult learning; and establishing feedback loops to assess if goals are being met

- ○ Facilitators attending to process as much as product/content; choosing, using, and adapting discussion-based protocols and other professional learning routines; setting schedules for professional learning; and rotating roles (e.g., notetaker, timekeeper, presenter of student work)

- ○ Designers adopting and treating instructional dilemmas as design problems, not as inherent deficiencies in teachers or students (e.g., how can we solve this problem?)

- ○ Advocates advocating for students; teachers; community partnerships; and practices, models, and programs

3. **Differentiating Professional Learning Experiences**

Effective literacy leaders strategically design professional learning to guide instrumental, socializing, and self-authoring experiences (Breidenstein, Fahey, Glickman, & Hensley, 2012), slowly guiding teachers to facilitate their own ongoing professional experiences. The Levels of Intensity outlined in the next section can help literacy leaders consider which kinds of professional learning experiences might be appropriate over time.

4. **Developing a Culture Conducive to Coaching**

Literacy leaders must always attend to building and managing school culture, as part of continually improving literacy teaching and learning. Looking carefully at Leana and Pil's (2006) framework of human and social capital allows a literacy leader to consider where content and pedagogical knowledge resides (human capital) and where patterns of interactions and relationships within and outside the school are strong (social capital). Thinking of school culture in this way allows literacy leaders to assess and build capacity (both human and social capital) through specific professional learning initiatives and routines.

USES

○ **Coach:** When organizing your yearly, monthly, and weekly schedule in conversation with colleagues and your school or district leadership team, you might use this framework to both explain your many roles and to make collaborative decisions about how best to spend your time.

○ **Principal:** When talking with your coaches, keep this framework handy as a way of guiding conversations, assessing specific aspects of coaching work, and continually seeking a balanced approach to schoolwide improvement in literacy teaching and learning.

REFLECTION

○ **Coach:** As a coach, which ways of thinking and working come most naturally to you? Which are easiest to adopt in your current role? Which ways of thinking and working may you need to adopt in the near future? What conversations might you need to have with your principal and colleagues in light of this framework?

○ **Principal:** As a formal leader, which ways of thinking and working like a coach have you already adopted? Which might you need to adopt soon? How might you best support your coaches in developing the habits of mind and skills they need to succeed in their roles?

NOTES FROM THE AUTHORS

JI: This framework grew very much out of Rita's and my experiences as school- and district-based instructional coaches, as well as our own research and understanding of the coaching literature. We believe that these four dimensions, when taken together, provide both coaches and formal school leaders with a way of understanding and organizing coaching work.

RB: When Jacy and I developed this framework, I thought back to my experiences as a coach, and realized how helpful it would have been to see and understand the importance of these four dimensions of effective coaching. At that time, I was learning on the job! Luckily, I was working with principals and teachers who supported me in my work, and they were eager to learn all they could about effective literacy instruction. We were learning together.

CHAPTER 2

Levels of Intensity

Coaches should consider how they might differentiate coaching activities for individuals and groups of teachers by considering how formal or intense the activities are. Activities can be categorized by three levels of intensity.

- **Level 1: Building Relationships (Informal/ Less Intense).** Coaches engage in these activities as a means of developing relationships in which teachers become comfortable with coaching and the coach.

- **Level 2: Analyzing Practice (Semi-Formal/ Slightly More Intense).** Coaching is now focused on improving literacy instructional practices (e.g., coaches and teachers working together to analyze data, lessons, or student work; co-planning lessons).

○ **Level 3: Transforming Practice and Making Teaching Public (Formal/Intense).** Coaching is focused on changing or transforming practices through modeling, co-teaching, or observing. Teachers and coaches are engaged in activities where they think critically about their own practices, assumptions, and beliefs.

Figure 2.1 provides a list of activities that fall within each of the three levels. Consider how these might differentiate coaching for various individuals and groups of teachers.

Level 1: Building Relationships
(Informal/Less Intense)

- ○ Having conversations with colleagues (getting to know one another, identifying issues or needs, setting goals, problem solving)
- ○ Establishing schedules for meeting with groups of teachers and individuals
- ○ Establishing norms for collaboration and conversation
- ○ Developing and providing materials for or with colleagues
- ○ Developing curriculum with colleagues
- ○ Participating in professional development activities with colleagues (conferences, workshops)
- ○ Leading or participating in study groups
- ○ Assisting with assessment of students

- Instructing students to learn about their strengths and needs
- Coaching on the fly (having unscheduled, brief meetings with teachers that provide opportunities for additional coaching)

Level 2: Analyzing Practice

(Semi-Formal/Slightly More Intense)

- Having conversations with individual colleagues about teaching, learning, and literacy (analyzing data, lessons)
- Co-planning lessons
- Revisiting norms for collaboration and making certain they facilitate group work
- Introducing discussion-based protocols to assist in the analysis of student work, the holding of group conversations about student/teacher work, and so on, which require higher degrees of trust
- Holding team meetings (grade level, data, department)
- Analyzing student work to assist teachers in planning instruction
- Analyzing and interpreting assessment data (helping teachers use results for instructional decision making)
- Making presentations at professional development meetings
- Assisting with online professional development

Figure 2.1: Coaching activities (Levels of Intensity) of specialized literacy professionals.

continues →

Level 3: Transforming Practice and Making Teaching Public

(Formal/Intense)

- Having conversations focusing on co-planning, co-teaching, and teaching dilemmas
- Modeling and discussing lessons
- Co-teaching lessons
- Expanding the range of discussion-based protocols used, including those that require higher degrees of risk/trust and surface assumptions related to issues of equity and social justice
- Helping individuals and groups design their own discussion-based protocols and collaboration routines
- Visiting classrooms and providing feedback to teachers as part of the planning/observation/debrief cycle
- Conducting individual and group analysis of videotaped lessons of teachers
- Engaging in lesson study with teachers
- Participating in and leading professional learning communities
- Providing support to teachers as a result of teacher performance evaluation outcomes
- Involvement in efforts to improve school literacy programs
- Facilitating school-community partnership work

Adapted from the following three sources: R. M. Bean, 2004; International Literacy Association, 2015; J. Ippolito, 2013.

The Levels of Intensity are a guide, not a prescription. They are not to be used in a linear fashion, from Level 1 through Level 3. They are to be used intentionally, with coaches thinking about which activities might work well at a specific time with a specific teacher or group.

Reasons for differentiating coaching activities are many:

○ Student needs—In some classrooms, students may need additional work with developing academic vocabulary; meanwhile, in other classrooms students may need additional work with decoding skills, etc.

○ Teacher readiness and preferences—To be effective, coaching requires developing a relationship of trust. Activities that develop such trust are identified in Level 1. Likewise, teachers may have some preferences for specific activities, that is, they may prefer the coach to model rather than to observe initially; they may want to co-plan rather than to co-teach.

○ System needs—Specific literacy skills may have been identified as a specific need for a grade level, school, or academic department (e.g., students' informational writing skills).

USES

- **Coach:** You might consider using the Levels of Intensity as a guide for keeping a record of your coaching activities. Such a record might be useful to share with the principal or administrator who has the responsibility of evaluating your work.

- **Principal:** The Levels of Intensity can be used as a conversation starter with your coaches. It can help you to develop a common language about coaching and aid you in understanding why a coach might focus their work with a specific grade at Level 1 and their work with another grade at Level 2 or 3.

REFLECTION

- **Coach:** As a coach, which activities do you feel most comfortable with? Which have you used most frequently? Which might be most effective in improving teaching practices in your school?

- **Principal:** At which levels do you see your coaches focusing their work? Does this focus meet the needs of the school, its teachers, and students? What next steps might you suggest to your coaches?

NOTES FROM THE AUTHORS

RB: Remember the expression often attributed to Mother Teresa: "I don't care what you know until I know that you care." Gaining a sense of trust is key. However, coaches who stay at Level 1 might find that teachers become too dependent on them. Transformational instructional improvement requires coaches to work at Levels 2 and 3.

JI: In my experience, adopting and adapting discussion-based protocols helps coaches move beyond Level 1 in ways that can feel safe and productive. Looking at the "Continuum of Discussion-Based Protocols" may help coaches and principals to choose and sequence protocols wisely (available at tinyurl.com/continuumofprotocols).

CHAPTER 3

School Culture: Considering Human and Social Capital

The culture of the school affects the success of coaching and, likewise, coaching can influence school culture. Two important constructs that influence organizational culture include human capital and social capital (Leana & Pil, 2006).

- ○ **Human Capital**—the human resources in the school (i.e., the experiences, backgrounds, beliefs, and knowledge of faculty, staff, and administrators)

- ○ **Social Capital**—subdivided as follows:

  - • **Internal:** patterns of interactions between and among individuals in the school (i.e., how well do they work together?). For example, do the staff share a common vision about literacy and learning?

• **External:** relationships of the school with its families and other agencies or organizations

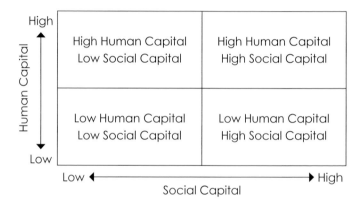

Figure 3.1: Human and social capital relationships.

USES

○ **Coach:** Figure 3.1 can be used to help you think about the school in which you work and how the culture of the school affects coaching decisions. You might want to talk with your principal and compare your views with theirs. You might also consider using this graphic with the staff in your school, helping them think about the culture of the organization as follows:

- Talk to teachers about each of the quadrants and what they mean. For example, the upper right quadrant represents schools in which there are experienced and effective teachers (high human capital) and these teachers work well together toward a common goal (high social capital).

- Ask teachers to individually place their school in one of the quadrants and then share their responses with others. How similar or different are the responses? What are the rationales for placement?

- Discuss whether there is a need to make changes in the school and how.

○ **Principal:** As the principal, you probably have a good understanding of your school's climate and how you might improve it. At the same time, your perspectives, especially as you think about the school as a whole (beyond the literacy program) might be different from that of the coach's. Use the graphic as a starting point for a discussion with your coaches about the status of the school and how to move forward with plans for improvement.

REFLECTION

○ **Coach and Principal:** Once you have used the graphic to think about the strengths and possible needs of your school, what do you think are the next steps? Each of you might identify some ideas for moving forward, and then discuss. For example, if teachers are knowledgeable and have many years of teaching experience (high human capital), but tend to work "behind closed doors," what could be done to change this behavior, to develop social capital?

NOTES FROM THE AUTHORS

RB: Changing the culture of a school from one that is toxic to one in which staff work together to address student learning is one of the most important tasks of coaches and principals. It can be done, but it is a journey that takes time and an all-out effort to develop a sense of ownership and responsibility among all staff in the school.

JI: School culture can be shifted by the collaborative efforts of school leaders, coaches, and teacher leaders working toward common goals. The more transparent leadership teams and teaching teams can be with each other, the more quickly cultural changes can be realized.

CHAPTER 4

Coaching Individuals

Three of the most common ways to work with individual teachers are modeling, co-teaching, and observation/ debrief cycles.

Modeling

When modeling instruction, coaches should be careful to:

- ○ establish clear goals

- ○ involve teachers as they model

- ○ talk and reflect with the teacher soon after the lesson

- ○ follow up with the teacher (including reversing roles, with the coach observing the teacher model).

Co-Teaching

Co-teaching can take many forms, including:

- one person teaching while the other assists
  (e.g., one adult leading the lesson while the
  other assists students)

- parallel teaching (e.g., each adult working with
  a different small group, generally on a similar
  concept or skill)

- station teaching (e.g., each adult facilitating
  center work while students rotate)

- turn taking or team teaching (e.g., adults
  coordinating efforts to teach a single lesson)

Observation/Debrief Cycle

At the heart of individual coaching work is the
observation and debrief cycle. Figure 4.1 shows four
main phases in a traditional cycle:

- Pre-observation conversation where the coach
  and teacher collaboratively establish a goal for
  the observation.

- Observation of instruction where the coach
  observes the teacher and students.

- Analysis of what was seen where the coach
  makes meaning of what was observed.

    ○ Post-observation conference in which the coach and teacher collaboratively make sense of the instruction and plan for next instructional steps.

    This observation cycle is foundational in establishing relationships with teachers and helping them to set and achieve their professional goals.

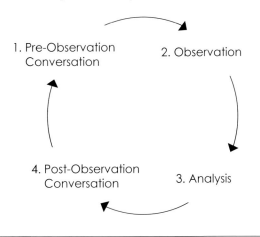

Figure 4.1: The Observation/Debrief Cycle.

USES

○ **Coach:** You might consider sequencing these practices differently with various colleagues. Some teachers may want to begin with modeling, move to observation, and finish with co-teaching. Others may need modeling, co-teaching, and then observing to refine the work. What do you find works best for you? What works best for the teachers you work with most often?

○ **Principal:** Supporting coaches in conducting observation cycles is critical to improving teaching and learning within and across classrooms. Whenever possible, resources should be allocated to support coaches in doing this essential, fine-grained instructional improvement work. At this point in time, how often are observation cycles occurring? What might you do to increase or bolster this work? At times, you may want to use a similar cycle when observing teachers, especially novices.

REFLECTION

○ **Coach:** As a coach, which of the three practices (modeling, co-teaching, observing) feels most comfortable to you? Which might you want to use more in your upcoming work?

○ **Principal:** As a principal, how are you supporting coaches and teachers who are engaging in this instructional improvement work? Which of these practices (modeling, co-teaching, observing) are you yourself adopting? In what ways are you, as a formal leader, working as a coach when you engage in formal and informal observation and evaluation cycles?

NOTES FROM THE AUTHORS

JI: Many coaches, early in their work, worry that they have not jumped into observation cycles immediately. It is important to remember that this kind of detailed work is built on a bedrock of strong relationships with teachers (and formal leadership). Keep inviting teachers to participate. Encourage your principal to make observation cycles a schoolwide priority and expectation. This work has a way of snowballing once it gets started and teachers see improved student learning as a result!

RB: Although it is important to understand how to use each of the activities described in this section, the key to successful coaching is effective communication. The language of coaching requires the ability to develop teacher reflectivity and a sense of inquiry. Effective coaches understand the value of and how to use paraphrasing, clarification, and elaboration as effective communication tools.

CHAPTER 5

Facilitation and Group Coaching

When facilitating the professional learning of small groups, literacy leaders are wise to consider various tasks and roles. One way to think about the work of group facilitation is to distinguish between *task roles* (focusing on achieving goals) and *maintenance or relationship-building roles* (focusing on building relationships and fostering collaboration) (Hersey & Blanchard, 1977; Johnson & Johnson, 2003). Following are seven general guidelines for facilitating group learning.

Guidelines for Working with Groups

- **Set norms for participation early and review them periodically.** Collaboratively establishing norms for professional engagement helps groups to name, own, and periodically review and revise how to work well with one another.

- **Be the "guide on the side."** As much as possible, facilitating group learning should allow for participants' voices and ideas to be front and center, with the facilitator guiding and shaping conversations; setting, achieving, and documenting group goals; helping to moderate differences of opinion; and helping the group reach consensus when possible.

- **Remember that engagement is important.** Full and active participation of everyone in the group is important. Even if not all members of the group participate in the *same ways* (e.g., some talking more, some offering student work, some taking notes), active participation and engagement are critical to long-term group success.

- **Balance routine and repertoire.** Consider how to balance *routines*—such as ways of connecting with one another, ways of sharing student work, ways of setting goals, and revisiting past topics—with *repertoire*, or the notion that each meeting should have something small that is different, surprising, or newly engaging (Wasley, Hampel, & Clark, 1997).

○ **Create an agenda.** Agendas are key to keeping a group on track for successful conversations. Agendas can help a facilitator move things along, while also keeping a consistent focus on the significant topics and goals.

○ **Make decisions in a group-appropriate way.** Decide early on, as a group, how decisions will be made. How important is complete consensus? Will voting be a part of the group's process? Making decision-making processes transparent and sticking to them will be of utmost importance, especially when the group disagrees.

○ **Differences are inevitable.** Differences of opinion in groups are inevitable—facilitators should expect and accept differences of opinion, using agreed-upon decision-making processes to resolve any tensions that arise. Sometimes tabling a conversation or setting up a side conversation with an individual can help defuse tensions.

Protocols and Resources Useful for Group Coaching

Consider the use of discussion-based protocols or other structured routines to help guide small-group learning. We have created a *Continuum of Discussion-Based*

Protocols (download from tinyurl.com/continuumof protocols), which gives facilitators some sense of a scope and sequence for discussion-based protocols. Sequencing protocols and introducing groups to low-stakes structures and routines first gives them time to build routines and relationships, before delving into riskier conversations and dilemmas. Facilitators might introduce protocols by having participants simply share experiences, then move to text-based discussions, then look at student work and data, and finally move into collaborative planning, addressing dilemmas, and discussing issues related to equity and social justice.

USES

- **Coach:** As an instructional coach, working with small groups is likely a major part of your role. If you are not currently setting norms, using agendas, and facilitating discussion-based protocols, explore some of the resources found on the School Reform Initiative's website (schoolreforminitiative.org) to see which tools you might adopt. If you are currently using these tools, consider how you might more effectively sequence the resources to grow your group's capacity to reflect, raise and solve instructional dilemmas, and surface hidden assumptions about teaching and learning.

○ **Principal:** These guidelines and resources for small-group coaching are completely applicable to the small-group work that principals often facilitate. Talk with your coaches about how you can better align small-group coaching and meeting practices across the school to build a common language and set of expectations about professional learning work.

REFLECTION

Coach and Principal:

○ As a participant in a group meeting, think about how the leader used the general guidelines presented above. What made the meeting effective? What changes might have enhanced the work of the group?

○ After leading a small group meeting, think about how you used the guidelines described above and how they supported your facilitation of that meeting. What would you change and why?

○ After a small-group meeting for which you were the leader, ask participants to respond to two questions: How comfortable were you in raising issues or presenting ideas? What activities were used in the meeting that made it a productive one?

NOTES FROM THE AUTHORS

JI: Norms, agendas, and protocols—the combination of this trinity revolutionized my own coaching and literacy leadership work. The three related tools and processes make the work transparent, keep groups on task, and allow us to have deeper and more meaningful conversations in shorter amounts of time.

RB: Group work can be a powerful means of improving the overall culture of a school. It is also an efficient way of supporting teacher learning. However, facilitating groups can be stressful if leaders and participants don't understand how to work effectively in a group. Taking the time to develop a group's understanding of how to work effectively is important (e.g., developing group norms).

CHAPTER 6

Assessment as a Guide to Student Literacy Learning

The topic of assessment is probably one of the most frequently discussed among school leaders and often one of the most contentious. Issues about which assessments to use, how to interpret results, and with whom to share interpretations can consume the time and energy of many literacy leaders. Literacy leaders have an important task, that of developing an assessment culture in which educators understand basic principles of sound assessment practices and use the process and results appropriately (Stiggins, 2014).

Purposes of Assessment

Assessment tools should provide both formative and summative data, useful for informing instruction and for accountability purposes. School personnel are better informed when they have multiple sources of data available to them, from the more informal (e.g., student observations, looking at student work samples, and teacher-made tests) to the formal (e.g., standardized tests given annually, benchmark measures). Students can also be involved in self-assessment (for additional sources of data, visit tinyurl.com/CCMSourcesofData).

Importance of an Assessment System

Literacy leaders have an important responsibility—that of leading efforts to design an assessment system that provides multiple measures of student learning, and at the same time, assisting teachers in understanding how to interpret and use the results for instructional planning. Important questions to ask about an assessment system include:

○ Are the assessments consistent with the goals and outcomes identified as most critical for literacy development at various grade levels?

○ What is the major purpose of each assessment tool?

○ Are all components of literacy learning represented (e.g., reading, writing, communication)?

○ At the same time, are just the critical components for specific grade levels or subjects measured (i.e., have redundancies and overtesting been eliminated)?

○ Do the assessments provide measures of student learning over time?

Using Data to Improve Classroom Instruction

Literacy leaders can facilitate teachers' work with data by participating in or leading data-team meetings. Assessment results serve as the focus for these collaborative problem-solving sessions. Generally, teachers either prepare or are provided with data (from the literacy coach or principal) about the students in their grade level or subject areas. They use this information for making decisions about the strengths and needs of students, and most importantly, for informing instruction. Table 6.1 provides a summarized protocol for a data meeting.

Table 6.1: Protocol Summary

Guiding Questions: What are the key points to consider?
Data Analysis: What do the data suggest about student strengths and needs?
Group Interpretation: What do the data mean for instruction, grouping, additional assessments?
Action Steps: Who will do what and when? How? How can literacy leaders be helpful?
Follow-up: How do we prepare for the next meeting? Any assignments?

Download a printable version of the full protocol here: **tinyurl .com/datamtgprotocol**

Limitations and Pitfalls

Too much focus on assessment can lead to a narrowing of the curriculum or even reduce the amount of time spent on instruction. Criticism about the emphasis on assessment for its effect on student stress and anxiety has been raised by both teachers and parents.

USES

○ **Principal and Coach:** Principals and coaches can use the questions in this booklet to guide them as they work with district leadership in the development of a coherent assessment system that is streamlined and comprehensive. They can also use the protocol above to facilitate data-team meetings.

REFLECTION

○ **Principal and Coach:** Use the questions above to think about the assessment system in your district or school. Is it a coherent, comprehensive one? How can it be improved? Which of the assessments in your school or district provide meaningful information and are used by teachers to inform instruction? What professional learning experiences do teachers need to better understand the value and limitations of the assessments they use?

NOTES FROM THE AUTHORS

RB: Too often, teachers at all levels feel compelled to prepare students for upcoming standardized tests instead of instructing them. I'm hoping that we are now seeing a shift in this practice.

JI: Coaches can play an integral part in helping to collect, organize, and lead the interpretation of literacy data in a school. However, principals and coaches must be careful not to neglect other coaching roles and responsibilities (e.g., conducting observation cycles, facilitating professional learning communities, etc.) in exchange for more and more data work!

CHAPTER 7

Developing a Schoolwide Literacy Plan

In *Cultivating Coaching Mindsets*, we emphasize the importance of a dual focus for coaches, working simultaneously with individuals and the system. Effective schools are ones in which there is a focused, schoolwide effort to work toward common goals, with all individuals working collectively in ways that ensure these goals are achieved. Principals and coaches can work collaboratively with teachers to develop a schoolwide literacy plan in which goals and action steps are developed, implemented, and sustained over time. By developing a literacy leadership team, principals and coaches can develop the collective capacity of teachers and a sense of ownership of the literacy program.

Literacy Leadership Teams

The literacy leadership team should include representative groups of teachers; for example, members might represent specific grade levels, those who teach various subgroups of students, or teachers of the disciplines. Ideas for working with the literacy leadership team follow:

○ Work with the group to establish efficient ways (surveys, interviews) to obtain input from stakeholders (e.g., other teachers, families, students) about the literacy program.

○ Establish a list of questions for teachers to consider when thinking about the strengths and weaknesses of the literacy program (download a list of possible questions here: tinyurl.com/QuestionsfromCCM).

○ Consider implementing a needs assessment process to facilitate the development of the literacy plan. Such a process can have a narrower focus (e.g., in what ways is literacy being used in service of disciplinary learning at middle and secondary levels?), or it can be more comprehensive, addressing the entire literacy program (e.g., across elementary grade levels).

○ Consider data from several different sources. Bernhardt (2013) describes four broad areas:

- Demographics: students and their families, enrollment, attendance

- Student Learning: formative and summative assessment measures

- Perceptions: attitudes; values; beliefs of teachers, families, and students

- School Processes: programs, instructional processes

The Comprehensive Literacy Program: Planning for Action

A needs assessment tool should lead to the development of a schoolwide literacy plan that includes strategies for action. A key step is to establish priorities and a plan for accomplishing them. Too many initiatives can be frustrating and confusing. An action plan should include the following: goals, their priority, action steps (who will do what), and a time line. Other essential components of the action plan are: resources needed, lead person(s), and evidence about implementation and evaluation (view and download an action planning guide here: tinyurl.com/actionplanningguide).

Five key points to consider when developing and implementing a comprehensive literacy plan are:

○ It is a journey that occurs over time and will include detours and roadblocks, but it can be a rewarding and worthwhile set of experiences (download a list of possible roadblocks and solutions here: tinyurl.com/ Roadblocks-Solutions).

○ If the plan is written but not disseminated and implemented, it has little value (except perhaps for those who served on the team).

○ Writing the plan may be challenging, but the implementation stage is the most difficult of all (Jerald, 2005, p. 2), given that it often involves transformational change and adaptive challenges. Implementation requires the thoughtful leadership of both principals and coaches.

○ Teachers need adequate support and recognition for their implementation efforts.

○ Regardless of how structured a plan might be, no doubt it will be modified to fit the local context; in other words, "local expertise, capacity, and sophistication in project implementation, as well as local motivation and management style will affect implementation" (McLaughlin, 1990, p. 12).

USES

○ **Coach and Principal:** Both the coach and principal need to be involved in leading any comprehensive planning efforts. Use the suggestions above for organizing and leading a literacy leadership team. Coaches and principals might want to identify possible sources of data that may be useful and make them accessible to team members.

REFLECTION

○ **Coach and Principal:** What sorts of data are available in your school or district—and how readily available are they? What are your thoughts about the possible priorities for improving schoolwide literacy learning? Would it be the curriculum and its vertical alignment? The instruction available to meet the needs of all groups of students? The standards? Or perhaps the assessment tools used to make decisions about instruction?

NOTES FROM THE AUTHORS

RB: Coaches, principals, and teachers indicated that discussions about a comprehensive plan (and the possible needs of their school) helped them think about difficult issues that were often avoided as they went about their day-to-day tasks. They admitted that, though difficult, the task was a valuable one.

JI: A comprehensive plan for literacy instruction and improvement provides schools with a way of looking back and determining whether, when, and to what extent goals are being met. Then a revised plan can be crafted to move forward productively and with evidence/data in hand.

CHAPTER 8

Advocating for Strong Community Relationships

Oftentimes literacy leaders focus (rightly) on the teachers and students within their school building. However, this focus can sometimes become extreme and lead to tunnel vision that unintentionally neglects the powerful contributions of the wider community surrounding a school. Savvy literacy coaches, principals, and specialized literacy professionals understand that they must adopt the mindset of *advocate* and continually call for stronger school-community relationships. These stronger relationships can then be leveraged to bolster literacy learning within and outside of the schoolhouse.

One of the first steps in advocating for strong school-community partnerships is to conduct a needs assessment and self-assess the current state of affairs. Questions that literacy leaders might ask include:

- ○ Do we welcome families into our school by greeting them with enthusiasm and providing an atmosphere that shows our support of their presence?

- ○ Do we treat families with respect?

- ○ Do we use the expertise of families to help us do our job more effectively?

- ○ Do we use many ways to engage families in helping their children learn?

- ○ Do we as staff believe that we can improve student learning by engaging families?

Adapted from the following source: S. M. Constantino, 2008.

Once a needs assessment has been completed by a literacy leadership team, then coaches, principals, and other specialized literacy professionals might design small community-based projects that could strategically grow stronger school-community partnerships. Community-based partners might include local universities, preschool providers, local libraries, and grant-writing experts.

Examples of some productive school-community literacy-based projects include:

- ○ Library-school partnerships in which students travel to a nearby public library to acquire library cards, learn about the resources available, and sign up for ongoing book clubs and reading challenges. Librarians can also come to the school to lead book discussions and promote lifelong reading.

○ Bookmobile or Little Free Library partnerships in which community members support the distribution of free (or very inexpensive) books via creative means such as bookmobiles or "Little Free Libraries" (perhaps that students co-construct with community members).

○ Volunteer buddy reading partnerships in which senior citizens and other community volunteers enter the school on a regular basis to partner with young children as "reading buddies."

○ Read-a-thons sponsored by families and hosted in the school, in which the entire community comes together to engage in collaborative reading challenges.

○ Writing contests, essay workshops, and bookmaking events in which local community members support students' creation of new texts. This might be aimed at younger students creating art books with some writing, or it might be aimed at older students who need editors to provide feedback as they work on college application essays.

These are just a few of the school-community partnerships we have seen literacy leaders effectively spearhead in their schools and communities. Below we highlight a few reminders of what successful literacy leaders do when they act as advocates for stronger school-community partnerships.

Ways That Successful Leaders Advocate

- Find multiple ways to communicate with families (e.g., surveys, email, social media, backpack express, community gatherings, parent workshops, family English learner services).

- Provide activities and programs that support families in their efforts to guide their children's learning (e.g., open houses and parent-teacher conferences that teach parents about assessments and instructional approaches; student-led conferences; clear policies and procedures around homework and summer reading/writing initiatives; family liaisons and resource centers for families to connect with directly; family educational services).

- Involve families in decision making and encourage their participation as partners in efforts to educate their children (e.g., involving parents in decisions about homework, after-school clubs, parent-teacher organizations and networks).

○ Develop teachers' understanding of how to talk with and support families (e.g., literacy leaders developing mini-workshops for teachers about how to effectively communicate with families; collaborative parent-specialist-teacher conferences to make sure all parties are in the conversation).

USES

○ **Coach and Principal:** Conduct a brief, collaborative needs assessment related to school-community partnerships. Start with the questions outlined at the beginning of this section. What are your school's strengths? What are the needs? What might be a small win that could be a good entry point to more robust school-community relations around literacy teaching and learning?

REFLECTION

○ **Coach and Principal:** What has been your most successful school-community partnership in the past three years, as related to literacy teaching and learning? What made it so successful? Which community members or organizations are best-positioned to involve in a new venture? How might all new endeavors build upon and strengthen current successful initiatives? To what degree does your school or district have a well-developed systemic plan for school-community partnerships?

NOTES FROM THE AUTHORS

JI: When working as a building-based literacy coach, I was involved in supporting local college students and senior citizens who volunteered in our school as reading buddies. We also sponsored regular family literacy nights and bookmaking sessions for students of all ages. We asked poets and playwrights to come into our school to talk about their art with students. These small ways of engaging the community paid huge dividends in terms of student learning and fostering a wider culture of literacy in our community.

RB: In working in and with schools, I learned that one of the most effective ways of involving families was to hold events that involved their children. Attendance was high when children were putting on a play, reading short selections, or sharing what they had written for an audience. I also found that parents who served as volunteers became more respectful of teachers and the school (developing a better understanding of the challenges facing teachers). The children of these volunteers were proud that their parents were in school (e.g., reading to children, providing a helping hand to the teacher, or helping in the school library).

CHAPTER 9

The Coach and Principal Working Together

Many studies have found that coaching and coaches can be effective only when principals support and understand the coaching role (Bean, Dole, Nelson, Belcastro, & Zigmond, 2015; Bean & Lillenstein, 2012; Matsumura, Sartoris, Bickel, & Garnier, 2009). Further, there is strong evidence that school change and improvement occur when principals operate from a shared leadership perspective (Spillane & Diamond, 2007), that is, they strive to build the capacity of all staff to function as a team, share a common vision about how to improve literacy instruction, learn with and from teachers, and hold high expectations for students in the school. It is important then to cultivate a strong working relationship between coach and principal.

The coach-principal relationship may differ, depending on the principal's knowledge of literacy instruction, professional experience, and leadership stance. Principals with a strong literacy background may want to take the lead in thinking about how to improve the literacy program. However, frequently, principals will ask the coach to assume that responsibility. If this is the case, there will need to be frequent communication and sharing of ideas so that the principal is deeply involved and knowledgeable about all change efforts. In a recent study, Bean, Dagen, Ippolito, and Kern (n.d.) found that most frequently, principals indicated they shared the leadership with their coaches and accepted their recommendations about literacy instruction and the literacy program.

Assess your own coach-principal relationship by responding to the following questions. (We encourage principals and coaches to respond individually and then share/discuss the results.)

Coach-Principal Relationship Questionnaire

Have the coach and principal talked about coaching roles and responsibilities and shared ideas with teachers?

Yes / No / Somewhat

Suggestions

○ Collaboratively define coaching roles and responsibilities. Often each school's context affects the ways in which a coach's workload is determined. For example, in schools with many novice teachers, coaches may need to focus on helping them gain a better understanding of literacy instruction. But coaches and principals need to agree on this. Are coaches expected to work with individual teachers based on "request," or are coaches expected to work with *all* teachers in rotating cycles? Discuss the fact that all teachers in the school can benefit from coaching; in fact, coaching should not be seen as only for teachers experiencing difficulties. Schools that are just beginning coaching work might start with volunteers, but over time, all teachers should be involved in coaching work.

○ Based on factors such as number of teachers, human and social capital, coach experience, etc., collaboratively develop and share a plan for how coaches are expected to function (e.g., rotating coaching cycles with grade-level teams of teachers).

○ The principal and coach can lead a schoolwide meeting with teachers to discuss the coach's roles and responsibilities. One key is to emphasize the non-evaluative nature of the coaching role!

Do the principal and coach have a communication plan in which they talk on a regular basis?

Yes   /   No   /   Somewhat

Suggestions

- Arrange for a regularly scheduled meeting (weekly or bi-weekly). Develop a plan based on what works for the two of you (e.g., electronic communication, face-to-face, both).

- The coach might submit regular, brief one-page summaries of coaching work (a concise summary that addresses the main points).

- As the principal, encourage and facilitate communication with the coach. At times, the coach might be hesitant to bring up dilemmas or challenges.

- Maintain teacher confidentiality in terms of difficulties that individual teachers are experiencing. At the same time, bring up any issues that affect the overall literacy improvement of students. For example, "Test and observational data indicate that students at the third-grade level would benefit from more explicit vocabulary instruction. Here are some ideas that I think may be helpful."

○ Maintain principal confidentiality, or in other words, anything discussed in the principal's office stays in the principal's office.

Do the two of you share key information, making certain that each is aware of the major challenges and successes in the school and how they are addressed?

Yes / No / Somewhat

Suggestions

○ As the coach, share a workload schedule with your principal and the specifics of what you are working on. This involves providing a summary of how you are working with individuals and groups of teachers.

○ Be honest with the principal about any challenges you face (e.g., ongoing workload arrangements, or being taken away from coaching responsibilities frequently to substitute for teachers who are absent).

○ Remember, *no surprises*! Coaches and principals should update each other about new or ongoing initiatives, as well as any difficulties or issues that have arisen.

Do the coach and principal work collaboratively to establish and then achieve a vision for literacy in the school?

Yes / No / Somewhat

Suggestions

- Both of you can share up-to-date information by discussing what you have learned at conferences or by sharing articles about literacy instruction and assessment. Consider highlighting important points or summarizing articles.

- The coach might make suggestions about how the principal can support initiatives that focus on achieving specific literacy goals.

- The principal should, when possible, attend team meetings and professional learning activities. If the principal cannot attend, the coach might summarize what was discussed at the meeting and share handouts and evaluation comments.

Does the coach respect and value the perspectives of the principal in terms of leading school efforts to improve student learning?

Yes / No / Somewhat

Does the principal respect and value the work of the coach?

Yes   / No / Somewhat

Suggestions

- As a coach, acknowledge the importance of the principal and how they can help you to become a better coach. Publicly and privately express your appreciation for the support of the principal.

- Acknowledge that the principal brings a different lens to school improvement and student learning. The principal's perspective can give you different, and often broader, insights into what is needed to improve teaching and learning.

- As a principal, acknowledge the importance of the coach and how they can help you to become a better principal. When principals provide coaches with positive feedback and show respect for the importance of their work, they provide coaches with the support needed to move forward with confidence. Coaching is not an easy job; teachers are accustomed to working in isolation, and the role of the coach is often ambiguous and can be perceived by teachers as interfering. Principals can help coaches become more self-confident in their role. Moreover, principals are best-positioned to shape how teachers in a school building perceive and work with coaches.

Final Thoughts

There may be times when the two of you—coach and principal—may not share the same perspectives about the school's literacy program or plans for school improvement. Given the differences in your positions and responsibilities, some differences of opinion are inevitable. However, if the two of you build a strong, trusting, and respectful relationship, such issues can be discussed openly and honestly. Finally, remember that shared leadership requires all those in a school to work together to facilitate student learning. The myth of a superhero leader working alone (either the coach or the principal) is just that—a myth.

USES

○ **Coach and Principal:** We encourage the coach and the principal to think about their responses to the items on this questionnaire. Depending on your comfort level, you may also decide to discuss your responses with each other. Regardless, we hope you will use some of the suggestions above to improve the relationship you have with each other.

REFLECTION

○ **Coach and Principal:** Now that you have responded to the questions above, what are the strengths of your coach-principal relationship? Where might it be improved? What one thing might you do to improve the relationship in the short term? Long term?

NOTES FROM THE AUTHORS

RB: I have talked with coaches working in many different schools. All of them, without exception, mention the importance of principals and how their leadership is key to improving the literacy program and to the effectiveness of the coach. Moreover, when principals and coaches have a less than positive relationship, there is little likelihood that coaching will be effective.

JI: I have always seen the coach-principal relationship as a strong indicator of the overall health of coaching work in a school. In schools with a strong coach-principal relationship, teachers have a clearer sense of literacy improvement goals and processes. In schools with a weak coach-principal relationship, teachers are often unclear about coaching purposes and approaches. If a shared coach-principal vision can be crafted and shared widely, then coaching work will be far more effective than if the coach is going it alone.

References

Bean, R., & Lillenstein, J. (2012). Response to intervention and the changing roles of schoolwide personnel. *The Reading Teacher*, *65*(7), 491–501.

Bean, R. M. (2004, Spring). Promoting effective literacy instruction: The challenge for literacy coaches. *The California Reader*, *37*(3), 58–63.

Bean, R. M., Dole, J. A., Nelson, K. L., Belcastro, E., & Zigmond, N. (2015). The sustainability of a national reading reform initiative in two states. *Reading and Writing Quarterly: Overcoming Learning Difficulties*, *31*(1), 30–55.

Bean, R. M., & Ippolito, J. (2016). *Cultivating coaching mindsets: An action guide for literacy leaders*. West Palm Beach, FL: Learning Sciences International.

Bernhardt, V. L. (2013). *Data analysis for continuous school improvement* (3rd ed). New York, NY: Routledge.

Breidenstein, A., Fahey, K., Glickman, C., & Hensley, F. (2012). *Leading for powerful learning: A guide for instructional leaders*. New York, NY: Teachers College Press.

Constantino, S. M. (2008). *101 ways to create real family engagement*. Galax, VA: ENGAGE! Press.

Hersey, P., & Blanchard, K. (1977). *Management of organizational behavior: Utilizing human resources* (3rd ed.). Englewood Cliffs, NJ: Prentice-Hall.

International Literacy Association. (2015). *Multiple roles of specialized literacy professionals: Position statement.* Newark, DE: Author.

Ippolito, J. (2013). Professional learning as the key to linking content and literacy instruction. In J. Ippolito, J. F. Lawrence, & C. Zaller (Eds.), *Adolescent literacy in the era of the Common Core: From research into practice* (pp. 235–249). Cambridge, MA: Harvard Education Press.

Jerald, C. (2005). *The implementation trap: Helping schools overcome barriers to change* (policy brief). Washington, DC: The Center for Comprehensive School Reform and Improvement.

Johnson, D. W., & Johnson, F. P. (2003). *Joining together: Group theory and group skills* (8th ed.). Boston, MA: Allyn-Bacon.

Leana, C. R., & Pil, F. K. (2006). Social capital and organizational performance: Evidence from urban public schools. *Organization Science, 17*(3), 353–366.

Matsumura, L. C., Sartoris, M., Bickel, D. D., & Garnier, H. (2009). Leadership for literacy coaching: The principal's role in launching a new coaching program. *Educational Administration Quarterly, 45*(5), 655–693.

McLaughlin, M. W. (1990). The RAND change agent study revisited: Macro perspectives and micro realities. *Educational Researcher, 19*(9), 11–16.

Spillane, J. P., & Diamond, J. B. (Eds.) (2007). *Distributed leadership in practice.* New York, NY: Teachers College Press.

Stiggins, R. J. (2014). Improve assessment literacy outside of schools too. *Phi Delta Kappan, 96*(2), 67–72.

Wasley, P. A., Hampel, R. L., & Clark, R. W. (1997). *Kids and school reform.* San Francisco, CA: Jossey-Bass.